THE
FOLK DANCE BOOK

FOR ELEMENTARY SCHOOLS, CLASS ROOM, PLAYGROUND, AND GYMNASIUM

COMPILED BY

C. WARD CRAMPTON, M.D.

DIRECTOR OF PHYSICAL TRAINING
NEW YORK PUBLIC SCHOOLS

NEW YORK
THE A. S. BARNES COMPANY
1912

Stanhope Press
F. H. GILSON COMPANY
BOSTON, U.S.A.

PREFACE.

This book of folk dances is published for the sole purpose of placing in the hands of the teachers of the public schools and playgrounds in New York City a description and the appropriate music for the folk dances of the course of study and those which have been approved from time to time as good physical training procedure.

No attempt is made to justify their use or the grading which is used or suggested, nor is any scientific or theoretical end to be served by this collection. It is intended to be useful. All these dances have been used with success in this city and may be employed under like circumstances with the prospect of like success.

This collection is the result of the earnest and efficient work of the teachers of physical training and the class teachers in the New York City schools, whose devoted efforts have developed folk dancing in its legitimate sphere to the great benefit and joy of many thousands of children. It is in recognition of their fundamental part in the development of this phase of physical training, and on their behalf, that this book is issued.

Acknowledgment for descriptions of individual dances is made in the text. Especial recognition is due to the services of Miss Bessie K. Marsh, Miss Maud Edmunds, William H. Harper, Henry J. Silverman, and Harry Sperling, who have rewritten many dances; and to Miss Ellen Hope Wilson, who has assisted in collecting the material.

EDITOR.

CONTENTS

Part I

	Grade	Page
The Chimes of Dunkirk	1 a	1
Danish Dance of Greeting	1 b	2
Shoemakers' Dance	2 a	3
Children's Polka (Kinderpolka)	2 b	4
Vineyard Dance	3 a	6
English Harvesters Dance	3 ab	8
Tantoli	4 ab	10
Lassies' Dance. I (Kulldansen)	4 ab	11
Nixie Polka (Nigarepolska)	4 ab	12
Swedish Clap Dance (Klappdans)	5 ab	13
Bleking	5 ab	14
Finnish Reel	5 ab	16
Fryksdalspolska	6 a	17
Norwegian Mountain March	6 ab	18
Highland Schottische	6 ab	20
German Hopping Dance	6 ab	21
Hop, Mother Annika (Hopp Mor Annika)	7 ab	22
Swedish Ring Dance	7 ab	24
Ace of Diamonds	7 ab	25
The Irish Lilt	7 ab	26
The Oxen Dance (Oxdansen)	8 ab	30
Highland Fling	8 ab	34

Part II

	Grade	Page
Tailors' Dance	1–2	41
I See You	1–4	42
The Carrousel	1–4	44
German Clap Dance	1–4	45
The Rill. I	2–5	46
Nickodickomdij	4–6	47
Washing Song and Game	4–6	48
Chain Dance	4–6	50
The Irish Jig	5–8	52
Csárdás	5–8	55
Reap the Flax	5–8	56
Rheinlander	5–8	58
Lassies' Dance. II (Kulldansen)	6–8	60
A Russian Dance (Komarinskaja)	6–8	63
Mondanet Maganak	6–8	66
The Rill. II	6–8	69
Laudnum Bunches	7–8	70
Russian Cossack Dance	7–8	72
Swedish Polka (Fjällnäspolska)	7–8	74
Trallen	7–8	77
Stuyvesant Dance	7–8	80

INTRODUCTION.

Folk dances have come to fill an important place in physical training. They range in character from the simple song play in which the accompanying action may be descriptive of some trade to the highly developed collection of movements which are not descriptive of anything in particular, save the pure joy of life in rhythmic exercise. In varying degrees are found the elements of song, play, drama, and vigorous muscular work. For our purpose, it is necessary to make a careful choice of material, as many dances are very evidently inappropriate for scholastic and administrative reasons.

Folk dances should serve only their legitimate purpose, viz: recreation and other results supposed to be derived from informal gymnastics. Of course, no one expects that the educational, corrective, and disciplinary results which we can best obtain from formal gymnastics, will ever be supplied by the folk dances, nor do we wish them to subserve the functions of athletics, athletic games, or even aesthetic dancing. They supply a charming addition to our physical training procedure and we can expect large results from their intelligent use.

PART I

THE CHIMES OF DUNKIRK.

Formation.   Single circle.   Partners face each other, hands on hips.

Measures 1–2.   Stamp three times, — right, left, right.

Measures 3–4.   Clap three times.

Measures 5–8.   Join hands with partner and turn around in place with running steps, starting with left foot.

Measures 9–16.   Running steps.   Partners may be changed by moving forward on the last measure.

Repeat from beginning.

DANISH DANCE OF GREETING.

Formation. Single circle. Partners face centre, hands on hips.

Measures 1-2. Clap hands twice, turn to partner and bow. Turn to centre. Repeat, bowing to neighbor.

Measure 3. Stamp right, stamp left.

Measure 4. Turn around in place with four running steps.

Repeat from beginning.

Measures 5-8. Join hands in circle. Run sixteen steps to the right. Turn and run sixteen steps to left.

Repeat from beginning.

SHOEMAKERS' DANCE.

Formation.   Double circle.   Partners face each other.

Measures 1–2.   With arms shoulder high and hands clenched, roll one arm over the other three times.   Reverse and roll three times.   "Winding the thread."

Measure 3.   Pull hands apart and jerk elbows backward twice.   "Pulling thread tight."

Measure 4.   Clap hands three times.

Repeat measures 1 to 4.   On measure 4 hammer the fists three times.   "Driving the peg."

Measures 5–8.   Join inside hands, outside hands on hips.   Skip around the ring. Simple polka may be used.

Repeat from beginning.

CHILDREN'S POLKA.

(KINDERPOLKA.)

Formation. Single circle. Partners face each other. Join hands, arms extended at sides, shoulder high.

Measures 1–8. Glide polka towards centre—slide, close, slide, close, three running steps in place. Repeat moving outward two measures. Repeat the whole step four measures.

Measures 9–12. Clap thighs with both hands. Clap own hands in slow time. Clap partners' hands three times in quick time. Repeat.

Measures 13–14. Point right toe forward, place right elbow in left hand, and shake finger at partner three times. Repeat left.

Measure 15. Turn complete circle right, with four jumps.

Measure 16. Stamp three times.

Repeat from beginning.

CHILDREN'S POLKA.

(KINDERPOLKA.)

VINEYARD DANCE.

Formation.   To music.

Measures 1–8.   March in and form circle.   Face centre.

Measures 9–16.   Make motion of digging and patting the ground.   Stamp three times — right, left, right, — placing hands on hips.   Repeat three times. The last time turn around (right) while stamping.

Measures 9–16.   Make motion of gathering grapes and placing them in baskets. Stamp as before, and form double circle facing centre.

Measures 17–24.   Skip forward four steps.   Skip backward four steps.   Skip forward to centre.   Hook partner's right arm and turn around once. Skip backward to place.   Finish facing partner.

Measures 25–32.   Walk forward eight steps, passing on partner's right.   Turn and walk back to place.   Repeat.   Finish by running off the floor.

ENGLISH HARVESTERS DANCE.

Formation. Single circle. Partners face forward, hands on hips.

Measures 1–8. Run forward sixteen steps. Turn about and run sixteen steps to starting position. Finish facing partners.

Measures 9–16. Hook right arms and run sixteen steps, couple turning in place. Hook left arms and repeat to position. Finish side by side, facing forward.

Measures 17–24. Partners join inside hands and run forward sixteen steps, the one on the inside turning in place, the one on the outside taking inside position. Run sixteen steps back to position. Finish inside partner behind, outside in front, partners' hands clasped over head.

Repeat from beginning.

TANTOLI.

Formation. Double circle. Partners face forward. Join inside hands, outside hands on hips.

Measures 1–8. Heel and toe polka, stamping on polka step. Begin with outside foot.

Measures 9–15. With hands on partners shoulders, hop waltz turning right. This may be taken without turning the first time, and with turning on the repeat.

Measure 16. Stamp three times.

Repeat from beginning.

LASSIES' DANCE. I.

(KULLDANSEN.)

Formation. Single circle. Partners face each other, hands on hips.

Measures 1–8. Place right toe forward, turn half turn to left and bow to neighbor. Reverse and bow to partner. Repeat three times.

Measures 9–12. Dance twelve kicking steps in place, beginning with left foot.

Measures 13–14. Clap own hands, join hands with partner, stamp, and turn in place with three running steps.

Repeat from beginning.

NIXIE POLKA.

(NIGAREPOLSKA.)

Formation. Single circle. Face centre. One in centre as leader. Hands on
    hips.

Measures 1–4. All take bleking step — spring feet forward alternately heel on
    floor, toe up. On last note clap hands once.

Measures 5–7. Leader runs twelve steps to meet a partner. Others in place.

Measure 8. Stamp twice.

Repeat, leader and partner facing. As leader turns to run to some other player,
    the partner follows, placing both hands on the leader's shoulders.
    Repeat until all are in line. The line may face about each time, alternat-
    ing leaders. In large classes it is well to start with two in the centre,
    each leading his own line.

SWEDISH CLAP DANCE.

(KLAPPDANS.)

Good

Formation. Double circle. Partners face forward. Join inside hands, outside hands on hips.

Measures 1–8. Polka step forward, beginning with outside foot — step, close, step; alternating feet.

Measures 1–8 (repeated). Heel and toe polka, bending backward on "heel," and forward on "toe."

Measures 9–12. Face partners and bow. Up. Clap three times. Repeat.

Measures 13–14. Clap partner's right hand. Clap own hands. Clap partner's left hand. Clap own hands.

Measure 15. Turn to left striking right hand against partner's.

Measure 16. Stamp three times.

Measures 9–16. Repeat.

Repeat from beginning.

BLEKING.

Formation. Single circle. Partners face each other. Join both hands.

Measure 1. Jump, right heel forward, right arm forward, elbow straight, left arm backward, elbow bent. Twist body slightly to left. Jump reversing the position — left heel and arm forward, right arm back. Slow time.

Measure 2. Continue three times—right, left, right,—in quick time, touching toe to floor.

Measures 3–8. Repeat step three times.

Measures 9–16. Hop waltz, swinging partner to right. Hop waltz may be taken in place the first time.

Repeat from beginning.

BLEKING.

FINNISH REEL.

Formation. Two parallel lines facing each other. Hands on hips.

Measures 1–8. Hop left, touch top of right toe at side. Hop left, touch right heel at side. Repeat other side. Repeat whole step three times.

Measures 9–12. Step forward right. Stamp forward left, heels together. Step backward left. Stamp backward right, heels together.

Measures 13–14. With three running steps partners change places, passing on right side. Face the center on four.

Measures 15–16. Repeat, returning to former places.

Repeat from beginning.

FRYKSDALSPOLSKA.

Formation.   Single circle facing left, hands joined.
Measures 1–8.   Twelve running steps.   Stamp on first step.   Repeat.
Measures 9–16.   Eight mazurka steps, left — stamp, extend, bend.
Repeat from beginning.

NORWEGIAN MOUNTAIN MARCH.

Formation.   Triangle.   One leader and two following.   Leader holds a handkerchief in each hand.   Those following grasp handkerchief in outside hands,
inside hands joined.

Measures 1–16.   Polka step forward, stamping on first step, eight times and
repeat.   Bend in direction of moving foot.

Measures 17–24.   Leader stamps once and moves backward with polka step under arms of other two.   Number two (on left) dances under number
one's right arm.   Number three turns around under number one's right
arm.   Leader (number one) turns under his own arm.   Repeat.

Repeat from beginning.

NORWEGIAN MOUNTAIN MARCH.

HIGHLAND SCHOTTISCHE.

Formation. Single Circle. Partners face each other. Left arm in half circle over head, right hand on hip.

Measures 1–4. (1). Touch right toe to right side, hop left. (2). Raise right in back of left knee, hop left. (3). Touch right toe to right side, hop left. (4). Raise right in front of left knee, hop left. (5–8). Schottische step to right — slide, cut, leap, hop. Repeat step starting to left, right arm up.

Measures 5–12. Partners hook right arms, left hands on hips. Starting with the left foot, three running steps, and hop, extending right foot. Repeat three times. Hook left arms and repeat the step starting with the right foot. Repeat twice. On the last measure run forward four steps to meet new partner. Instead of running schottische, step hop or hop polka may be used.

Repeat from beginning.

GERMAN HOPPING DANCE.

Formation. Single circle. Partners face each other, inside hands joined and held high, outside hands on hips, when moving outward. Reverse when moving inward.

Measures 1–8. Glide outward four times. Glide inward four times. Repeat.

Measures 1–8 (repeated). Glide outward four times. Hop in place four times. Glide inward four times. Hop in place four times, making complete turn away from partners. Finish in circle facing centre, all hands joined.

Measures 9–12. Run sideways right, eight steps, crossing left in front of right. Repeat moving left, starting with left foot.

Measures 13–16. Glide forward towards centre of circle four times. Glide backward four times.

Measures 9–12 (repeated). Partners facing each other, glide outward four times. Hop in place four times.

Measures 13–16 (repeated). Glide inward four times. Hop in place four times, making complete turn away from partners. Finish in circle facing centre.

HOP, MOTHER ANNIKA.

(HOPP MOR ANNIKA.)

Formation.   Double circle.   Partners face forward.   Join inside hands, outside hands on hips.

Introduction.   Bow to partners and take hands facing front.

Measures 1–4.   Walk around circle sixteen brisk steps.   Begin with outside foot. Swing the arms.

Measures 5–8.   Skip sixteen steps.   Swing the arms.   Finish facing partners.

Measures 9–12.   Stamp forward right.   Clap partner's right hand.   Clap own hands.   Repeat left.   Repeat step three times.   Finish facing forward.

Measures 13–20.   Polka around circle turning toward and away from partner.

Repeat from beginning, changing partners to the right on introduction.

SWEDISH RING DANCE.

Formation.   Double circle.   Partners face forward.   Inside hands joined, outside on hips.

Measures 1–4.   Balance step, forward outward, with outside foot.   Repeat with inside foot.   Swing the arms.   Repeat the step.

Measures 1–4 (repeated).   Run forward eight steps — quick time.   Turn toward partner and draw foot into third position.   Partners face in opposite directions.

Measures 5–6.   Balance step as at first, beginning with outside foot.   Move toward new partner.

Measures 7–8.   Partners bow to each other.

Repeat from beginning.

ACE OF DIAMONDS.

Formation.   Partners face each other, hands on hips.   In circle or in line.

Measures 1–8.   Clap hands, hook right arms, polka, stamping on first step, and turning in place.   Repeat, hooking left arms.

Measures 9–16.   Number one dances backward with four hop steps, number two follows, moving forward.   Repeat, number one moving forward, number two backward.

Measures 17–24.   Polka forward.

Repeat from beginning.

THE IRISH LILT.

The steps of this dance are arranged in order of difficulty, the easier first, as used in the public high schools of Greater New York. The order may be changed. Each step with its "break" can be done to any eight measures. Any formation.

STEPS.

1. Forward Rock.
2. Kick.
3. Toe and Heel.

4. Leg Twist and Kick.
5. Side Step.
6. Kick and Change.

Break — a connecting step.

Before teaching this dance the preliminary step, Sideward Rock, may be used to advantage to establish the rhythm.

SIDEWARD ROCK.

From position with heels together and hands on hips, on count one, hop and raise right leg sideways. On count two, hop and bring right leg under body and raise left leg sideways. One measure.

Repeat rapidly to music.

FIRST STEP — FORWARD ROCK.

Similar to 'Sideward Rock' except that plane of movement is changed from sideward to forward and back. On count one, hop with weight on left foot, raising right foot backward. On count two, hop on right foot and raise left foot forward, one measure.

Repeat up to twelve counts (six measures), always raising left foot forward and right foot backward.

After the twelfth count, by means of the 'Break' (one measure), bring the right foot forward and repeat the step with 'Break.'

BREAK.

On count one, spring and spread feet. On count two, spring and bring feet together again. On count three, hop and raise left leg backward. On count four, hop and kick left leg forward. Two measures.

Practise this movement thoroughly. After having learned it the 'Break' is not used as a separate step but is used to connect the various steps, and to connect the first and second halves of each step. For example, when the twelfth count in the first half of 'Forward Rock' is reached, the left foot

Described by Thomas J. Browne, Commercial High School, Brooklyn.

is forward in the air; the feet should then be spread (count one of the 'Break'), brought together again (count two), the right leg raised in back (count three), then brought forward (count four), ready to be placed on the ground for the first count of the second half of the 'Forward Rock,' which is done with the right foot forward. The same process is gone through with at the end of the step in order to bring the left leg in position to start the next step.

Second Step — Kick.

Two counts to each foot.

On count one, spring and raise left leg backward. On count two, spring and kick left leg forward outward. On count three, spring to left and raise right leg backward. On count four, spring and kick right leg forward outward.

Continue to twelfth count (six measures), then do 'Break' for four counts (two measures), then repeat step with 'Break.'

Third Step — Toe and Heel.

Four counts to each side. Twelve counts — six measures.

On count one, spring and face to right, stretching left leg backward, but to left of starting position and placing left toe on floor. On count two, spring and about face to left, rotating left leg and placing left heel where toe was. On count three, spring and face to front, placing left toe on floor near right foot. On count four, spring and kick left leg forward outward. On count five, spring and land on left leg, facing to left with right leg extended and toe on floor. On counts six, seven and eight, proceed as with left leg. On counts nine to twelve, repeat with left leg. Then 'Break' and start with right leg for twelve more counts (six measures) and 'Break.'

Fourth Step — Leg Twist and Kick.

Similar to the 'Toe and Heel' except that the toe and heel of extended leg are not placed on the floor. The pointing out of this similiarity will aid in teaching the step. Four counts to each side. Twelve counts — six measures.

On count one, spring and face to right, raising left leg backwards. On count two, spring and about face to left, rotating left leg, but keeping it pointed in same direction, with knee slightly bent. On count three, spring and place left toe near right foot. On count four, spring and kick left leg outward. On count five, spring to left foot and face to left, raising right leg backward. On counts six, seven and eight, same as with left leg. On counts nine to twelve, with right leg. Then 'Break' four counts — two measures. Repeat, starting with left leg.

Fifth Step — Side Step.

Eight steps to two counts — one measure, instead of four as in the other "steps." On count one, place left leg across in front of right leg and left foot on floor to right of right foot. On count two, place right foot to right of left foot, but in back. On count three, again move left foot past right to right. On count four, again move right foot past left to right. On count five, again move left foot past right to right. On count six, again move right foot past left to right. On count seven, again move left foot past right to right. On count eight, hop on left foot and slightly backward, swinging the right leg forward. On count nine, place right foot to left of left foot in front. On count ten, move left foot to left. On counts eleven to fifteen, proceed as in first seven counts, but toward the left, starting the right foot in front. On count sixteen, hop on right foot and swing left leg forward. On counts seventeen to twenty-four, as in first eight counts. Then 'Break' and bring right leg forward and proceed for twenty-four counts — twelve measures.

The idea in this step is to take short steps sideways very rapidly, changing direction every eighth count with a hop.

Sixth Step — Kick and Change.

On count one, spring and place left toe back of right heel. On count two, spring and kick left leg diagonally forward. On count three, spring and place weight on left foot and raise right leg backward. On count four, hop with left leg, and still hold right leg up in back. On count five, hop with left leg, and place right toe back of left heel. On count six, spring and kick right leg diagonally forward. On count seven, spring to right and raise left leg backward. On count eight, hop with right foot, holding right leg up in back. On counts nine to twelve, as in first four counts. Then 'Break,' and repeat, starting with right toe.

Each step should start to the left and continue for twelve beats. Then the 'Break' should come in for four beats bringing the right leg forward; the step then resumed for twelve counts starting to the right, and finishing with the 'Break,' preferably stamping with the left leg on the fourth count instead of swinging it forward.

THE IRISH LILT.

(SCOTCH AIR.—THE CAMPBELLS ARE COMING.)

THE OXEN DANCE.

(OXDANSEN.)

This dance had its origin in the beginning of the last century, when at the college in Karlstad, Sweden, the freshmen, nicknamed "Oxen," were made to perform the dance before the sophomores. Hence the name "The Oxen Dance."

Formation.   The dancers (A and B) stand facing each other about two steps apart, hands on hips.   If there are several dancers, they form two lines facing each other.

FIGURE 1.

(a). Measures 1–2.   At the beginning of the second measure A bows to B while B makes a deep courtesy to A.

Measures 3–4.   At the beginning of the fourth measure B bows to A while A makes a deep courtesy to B.

Measures 5–8.   Repeat.   These movements are done slowly.

Measures 9–16.   The bows and courtesies are continued in quicker time, one for each measure.

(b). Measure 17.   A places his clenched fist on chest, elbows at shoulder level, then throws the arms sideward, turns the head to right with a jerk.   At the same time the right leg is forcibly swung sideward with straight knee while he rises on the toes of his left foot, then he takes a long step to the right and places left foot beside the right.   The right foot is not placed on the floor until the third beat.

Measure 18.   A takes another short step to the right, stamps with left foot twice beside the right one, at the same time turning the head forward and gradually placing the hands on chest, elbows at shoulder level.

Measure 19.   A again extends his arms, turns head to left, swinging left leg sideward as described for the right, then takes a large step to the left and places right foot beside the left.   The left foot is not placed on the floor until the third beat.

Measure 20.   A takes a short step to the left and places right foot beside the left, turning head forward and placing hands on hips.

Measures 21–24.   Repeat.   B dances in the same way at the same time, but begins to the left side.

From SWEDISH FOLK DANCES by Nils Bergquist.

Figure 2.

(a). Measures 1–2.   At the beginning of the second measure both slide with a snap, left foot forward.

Measures 3–4.   At the beginning of the fourth measure both replace left foot and at the same time place right foot forward.

Measures 5–8.   Repeat.

Measures 9–16.   Continue the same movement in quicker time, the feet changing place twice in each measure.

(b). Measures 17–24.   Same as (b) in first figure.

Figure 3.

(a). Measures 1–2.   The dancers place right hands on tops of each other's heads, far back.   At the beginning of the second measure A pulls B's head forward.

Measures 3–4.   B raises his head and pulls A's head forward at the beginning of the fourth measure.

Measures 5–8.   Repeat.

Measures 9–16.   Continue same movement in quicker time, pulling and raising head twice during each measure.

(b). Measures 17–24.   Same as (b) in first figure.

Figure 4.

(a). Measures 1–2.   At the beginning of the second measure, both turn with a jump to the left — quarter circle — so that their right elbows touch.

Measures 3–4.   At the beginning of the fourth measure both turn with a jump to the right — half circle — and touch left elbows.

Measures 5–8.   Repeat.

Measures 9–16.   Continue same movement in quicker time, jumping twice during each measure.   At the last jump the dancers turn a quarter circle, facing each other again.

(b). Measures 17–24.   Same as (b) in first figure.

32

FIGURE 5.

(May be omitted.)

(a). Measures 1–2.   At the beginning of the second measure A sticks his fingers to his nose to B, while B grasps both ears and stretches out his tongue to A.

Measures 3–4.   At the beginning of the fourth measure B sticks fingers to his nose to A, while A grasps both ears and stretches out his tongue to B.

Measures 5–8.   Repeat.

Measures 9–16.   Continue same in quicker time, as in previous figures.

(b). Measures 17–24.   Same as (b) in first figure.

FIGURE 6.

(a). Measures 1–2.   At the beginning of the second measure A throws his right hand close to B's cheek as if to give him a box on the ears, B flinching as if struck, while B at the same time strikes his hands once down in front, then replaces hands on hips.

Measures 3–4.   At the beginning of the fourth measure B throws his right hand close to A's cheek, while A claps his hands once.

Measures 5–8.   Repeat.

Measures 9–16.   Continue same movement in quicker time, as described in previous figures.

(b). Measure 17–24.   Same as (b) in first figure.

THE OXEN DANCE.

(OXDANSEN.)

HIGHLAND FLING.

I.   Measure 1.   Touch right toe side right, hop on left.   Raise right in back of knee, hop on left.

Measure 2.   Touch right toe side right, hop on left.   Raise right in front of knee, hop on left.

Measures 3–4.   Repeat left.

Measures 5–6.   Repeat right.

Measure 7.   Break.   Leap onto right foot and quarter turn right.   Left foot in back of right knee.   Another quarter turn right, left foot in front of knee.

Measure 8.   Quarter turn right, left foot in front of knee.   Facing front, left foot in back of right knee.   One hand circled overhead, other on hip (side of active foot).

II.   Measure 9.   Leap onto right foot sideways, left raised sideways.   Left to right, right raised behind left knee, hop on right.

Measure 10.   Raise right in front of knee, hop on right.   Raise right in back of knee, hop on right.

Measures 11–12.   Repeat right.

Measures 13–14.   Repeat right, break right, turn right.

Measures 15–16.   Repeat same left side.

III.   Measure 1.   Touch right toe to right side, hop on left.   Raise in back of left knee, hop on left.

Measure 2.   Raise in front of left knee, hop on left.   Leap onto right raising left in back.

Measures 3–4.   Repeat left.

Measures 5–6.   Repeat right and break.

Measures 7–8.   Repeat same left side.

IV.   Measure 9.   Leap to right outward.   Raise left in back right knee, hop on right.

Measure 10.   Raise left in front right knee, hop on right.   Raise left in back right knee, hop on right.

Measures 11–12.   Repeat left.

Measures 13–14.   Repeat right and break.

Measures 15–16.   Repeat same left side.

V.   Measure 1.   Touch right toe diagonally forward, hop on left.   Raise right to front of left knee, hop on left.

Measure 2.   Touch left toe diagonally forward, hop on right.   Raise left in **front** of right knee, hop on right.

Measures 3–4.   Repeat left.

Measures 5–6.   Repeat right.

Measures 7–8.   Break, turning right.   Repeat, returning to original places.

VI.   Measure 9.   Touch right toe to right side, hop on left.   Leap to right and right raised to side right.

Measure 10.   Bend right knee and kick, hop on left.

Measures 11–12.   Repeat right.

Measures 13–14.   Repeat right.

Measures 15–16.   Break.   Repeat whole to left.

VII.   Measure 1.   Touch right toe to right side, hop on left.   Raise right in back of knee, hop on left.

Measure 2.   Touch right heel forward diagonally, hop on left.   Touch right toe to standing foot, hop on left.

Measures 3–4.   Repeat right.

Measures 5–6.   Repeat right.

Measures 7–8.   Repeat, end with break.

VIII.   Measure 9.   Stride jump.   Raise left in back of right knee, hop on right.

Measure 10.   In front, hop on right.   In back, hop on right.

Measure 11.   In front, hop on right.   In back, hop on right.

Measure 12.   In front, hop on right.   In back, turning to right.

Measures 13–16.   Right arm overhead four times, increasing tempo to finish.

HIGHLAND FLING. I.

HIGHLAND FLING. II.

PART II

TAILORS' DANCE.

A heart of happiness is mine,
To make a suit takes tailors nine;
A heart of happiness is mine,
To make a suit takes tailors nine.
With thimble, scissors, needle too,
And thread run through;
With thimble, scissors, needle too,
And thread run through.

Formation.   Single circle with chosen partners.

Measures 1–4.   All join hands and dance to left with skipping polka, as first two lines are sung.

Measures 5–8.   Left hands on hips, right arms raised, elbows level at shoulders, make motion of scissors with two first fingers; at same time touch left toe sideward, then point toe back.   Repeat.

Measures 1–4.   Partners dance around in place with four steps, accenting first step.

Measures 5–8.   Repeat above with left arm and right foot.

I SEE YOU.

I see you, I see you,
Ti-ralla-ralla-lalla-la!
I see you, I see you,
Ti-ralla-lalla-la!
You see me, and I see you,
And you take me, and I take you,
And you see me, and I see you,
And you take me, and I take you.

Formation. Two front columns of two ranks each, the columns facing each other. Those in the front ranks with the hands on the hips, those in the rear ranks with hands resting on the shoulders of those in front.

Measures 1–8. While singing, those in the rear ranks alternately bend their heads first to the left then to the right, thus playing "peek-a-boo" with the players in the opposite rear rank, at first slowly, i. e., twice on the first line, but four times on the chorus.

Measures 9–12. While singing the fifth line all clap hands sharply once, and those who have just been playing "peek-a-boo" run forward to the left of their neighbors in front, grasp hands with those from the opposite column, meeting them and swing around.

Measures 13–16. While singing the seventh and eighth lines change with a handclapping so that each dances with his original partner, and at the end quickly resume the formation in such a manner, however, that the former front ranks become rear ranks and vice versa, after which the play is repeated. (When danced vigorously it may be well to omit part of the song. EDITOR.)

By permission from SWEDISH SONG PLAYS by Jakob Bolin.

I SEE YOU.

THE CARROUSEL.

Pretty children, sweet and gay,
    Carrousel is running.
    It will run till ev'ning.
Little ones a nickel, big ones a dime.
Hurry up, get a mate, or you'll surely be too late.

CHORUS: — Ha—ha—ha, happy are we,
    Anderson, and Peterson, and Henderson, and me.
    Ha—ha—ha, happy are we,
    Anderson, and Peterson, and Henderson, and me.

Formation.   Form on two concentric circles, facing inward.

Measures 1–7.   The players of the inner circle grasp hands, those in the outer one placing their hands on the shoulders of those in front. Both circles move with followstep to the left.

Measures 8–9.   At the beginning of the chorus, the circles slide to the left.

Measures 10–11.   Then to the right.

Measures 8–11 (repeated).   Repeat to the left and to the right.

Repeat from beginning the circles now quickly changing places. (When danced vigorously it may be well to omit part of the song. EDITOR.)

By permission from SWEDISH SONG PLAYS by Jakob Bolin.

GERMAN CLAP DANCE.

Now with your hands go clap, clap, clap,
Now with your feet go tap, tap, tap,
Then have a care, my partner there,
Or in our fun you'll have no share.

Formation.   Form a circle of couples, boys' right and girls' left hands are joined, height of shoulders.

Measure 1.   March forward four steps.

Measure 2.   March forward four steps, clapping hands on first, second, and third beats.

Measure 3.   March forward four steps.

Measure 4.   Face each other and stamp — left, right, left — on first, second, and third beats.

Measure 5.   Cross point step forward right and raise right forearm, placing back of left hand under right elbow.   Shake right forefinger on first, second, and third beats.

Measure 6.   Change position and shake left forefinger on first, second, and third beats.

Measure 7.   Join right hands and form arch.   Complete turn left under arch.

Measure 8.   Stamp — left, right, left — on first, second, and third beats.

Measures 1–6 (repeated).   Repeat as above.

Measure 7 (repeated).   Clap both hands on thighs on one.   Clap hands on two.   Clap partner's hands twice on three and four.

Measure 8 (repeated).   Stamp — left, right, left — with shaking of head on first, second, and third beats.

From POPULAR FOLK GAMES AND DANCES, by Mari R. Hofer.

THE RILL. I.

One and two and three, four and five,
Now we again the Rill revive.
Dance we now the Rill all right,
And dance we now till it grows light.
Dance we now the Rill all right,
And dance we now from morn till night.

Formation.   Groups of fours.   Couple behind couple.   Partners join inside
    hands.   Join outside hands with rear couple.

Measures 1–4.   Two schottische steps forward beginning with outside foot.   All
    dance four jig steps (step, hop), the forward couple letting go of inside
    hands and passing to rear, and the rear couple moving forward to become
    the head couple.

Measures 5–8.   Repeat.

NICKODICKOMDIJ.

I.

Formation. Circle.

Measures 1–4. Couples dance eight schottische steps, beginning outside foot.

Measures 5–6. Partners take both hands and dance four bleking steps, starting left foot.

Measure 7. Partners turn one turn, A to left, B to right.

Measure 8. Both stamp with left foot, extend arms horizontally.

Measures 9–10. Partners clap own hands, then each others' twice.

Measures 11–12. Partners take hands and dance around in place. Repeat music.

II.

Measures 1–4. All dance "grand right and left."

Measures 1–4 (repeated). A swings meeting B on right arm in time with music.

Measures 5–6. Bleking steps.

Measure 7. Partners turn one turn.

Measure 8. Stamp left foot, extend the arms.

Measures 9–10. Partners shake warningly right hand index finger, then left.

Measures 11–12. Partners dance around in place.

WASHING SONG AND GAME.

I. We will wash our clothes, we'll wash them,
We will wash our clothes just see. :||

CHORUS. Tra, la, la, la, la, tra, la, la, la, la.
Tra, la, la, la, la, tra, la, la.

II. We will clap our clothes, we'll clap them.

III. We will rinse our clothes, we'll rinse them.

IV. We will wring our clothes, we'll wring them.

V. We will hang our clothes, we'll hang them.

VI. We will iron our clothes, we'll iron them.

VII. We will mangle our clothes, we'll mangle them.

Formation. Two lines facing, one step between.

I. Measures 1–4. Left hand, palm upward, is used as washboard. Rub right hand with closed fist on left palm, bending forward and up in time.

Chorus.

Measures 5–6. Hands on hips. Cross balance step to left, heels together.

Measures 7–8. Cross balance step to right.

Measures 9–10. Repeat to left.

Measures 11–12. All clap own hands, and marking the time by stamping turn once around in place.

II. Measures 1–4. B turns palms upward, A claps B's hands. Clap own hands. B claps A's hands. All clap own hands. Repeat.

Chorus. Measures 5–12. As above.

III. Measure 1. Partners hold each other's hands and swing the arms—first to A's left side.

Measure 2. Back in starting position.

Measure 3. To A's right side.

Measure 4. Back in starting position.

Measures 1–4. Repeat.

Chorus. Measures 5–12. As above.

IV. Measure 1. Partners join hands, B turns to right and A to left, raising outside hands overhead.

Measure 2. Back in starting position.

Measures 3–4. Repeat, turning other way.

Measures 1–4. Repeat from beginning.

Chorus. Measures 5–12. As above.

V. Measure 1. All stretch hands in front of chest.

Measure 2. Stretch arms overhead.

Measure 3. Lower arms sideward.

Measure 4. Hands on hips,

Measures 1–4. Repeat.

Chorus. Measures 5–12. As above.

VI. Measures 1–2. Join hands with partner in front, arms stiff. Odd couples run three steps and halt, A going backward, B going forward. Even couples run three steps and halt, A going forward and B backward,— all moving together. Return to place.

Measures 3–4. Repeat so that odd A's go forward and B's backward, and the even B's go forward.

Measures 1–4. Repeat.

Chorus. Measures 5–12. As above.

VII. Measure 1. Hands on hips, B bends knees, A bows.

Measure 2. Starting position.

Measure 3. A bends knees, B bows.

Measure 4. Position.

Measures 1–4. Repeat.

Chorus. Measures 5–12. As above.

CHAIN DANCE.

I am wandering here alone,
Looking for my playmate true;
I am wandering here alone,
Looking for my playmate true.
Come and see me meet him (her) here;
He (she) who is my playmate.
Will you, as you did before,
Swing and dance around with me?
Tra–la–la, la–la–la.

Can be danced by any number of couples, standing in ring, facing the centre, B on A's right side and B with right hand holding A's left hand, free hands on hips.

Measures 1–4. A faces to right and B to left, partners facing each other, couples dance with walking steps "grand right and left" and A steps in front of B whose right hands they are holding at end of fourth measure.

Measures 5–6. A and B, still facing each other and holding right hands, swing right arms in time with the song.

Measure 7. A, with left hand holding B's left and with right hand holding B's right, arms crossed, couples walk around the circle with four steps, a bow on each second step, B outside the circle and on A's right side.

Measure 8. Partners take both hands, arms extended horizontally, dance around in place with four walking steps.

Measures 9–10. A, holding B's left hand with right hand, free hands on hips, dance around the circle with two "pas de quatre" steps. Then partners holding both hands dance around in place with polka steps.

Measures 11–20. Repeat.

CHAIN DANCE.

THE IRISH JIG.

Formation.   Partners facing forward.   Hands on hips.

I.   Measure 1.   Stamp forward with outside foot.   Close with inside foot.
Measure 2.   Hop on inside foot, kick with outside foot, twice.
Measures 3–6.   Repeat twice with same foot.
Measures 7–8.   Hop on inside foot, point outside in fifth position.   Hop on outside foot, point inside in fifth position.   Repeat.   On last hop, turn facing partner.

II.   Measures 9–10.   With outside foot point forward four times, hopping on inside foot.
Measures 11–12.   Repeat, starting with inside foot.
Measures 13–14.   Repeat, pointing twice outward, and twice inward.
Measures 15–16.   Run forward two steps, turn and face partners on two steps. Bend body forward, clap in front of knees on first step.   Straighten on second step, hands on hips.
Measures 17–22.   Starting with inside foot, repeat foregoing step.
Measures 23–24.   Cross over, remaining back to back.
Measures 1–6.   Starting with outside foot, repeat.
Measures 7–8.   Turn three-quarter turn, finish facing front.

III.   Measures 9–10.   Jump backward. land on both feet.   Hop on right foot, kick with left foot three times.
Measures 11–12.   Repeat, hopping on left foot.
Measures 13–14.   Repeat, hopping on right foot.
Measures 15–16.   Repeat, hopping on left foot.   Finish facing partners.

THE IRISH JIG.

THE IRISH JIG. (Continued.)

IV.   Measure 17.   Spring sideways, with outside foot.   Place inside foot behind outside and raise outside foot.   Step in place with forward foot and raise rear foot.   Step in place with rear foot.

Measure 18.   Repeat in same direction.

Measure 19.   Repeat.

Measure 20.   Spring sideways with outside foot, hop on outside foot, and kick with inside.

Measures 21–24 and 1–8.   Repeat whole step three times, alternating directions. Finish facing forward.

V.   Measure 9.   Place outside heel forward, toe up.   Bring inside foot up to heel.   Snap outside toe down.

Measure 10.   Repeat, starting with inside foot.

Measures 11–12.   Four snatch steps backward — step hop.

Measures 13–24.   Repeat three times.

VI.   Measures 1–2.   Starting with outside foot, run forward four steps.

Measure 3.   Stamp forward, outside foot, point forward with inside foot.   Pushing with pointing foot turn a third of a turn outside and point forward.

Measure 4.   Repeat. Pushing with pointing foot and third of a turn, twice. Finish facing front.

Measures 5–7.   Six snatch steps backward, starting with inside foot.

Measure 8.   Stamp sideways toward partner.   Place outside toe behind inside heel and courtsey.   Stand.

CSÁRDÁS.

Formation. Single circle. Partners facing each other. Hands on partner's shoulders and hips.

Measure 1. Step towards the centre, close with outside foot, striking heels together. Repeat.

Measures 2–4. Repeat, moving away from the centre. Continue through the strain of music, alternating directions, four times in all.

Measures 5–12. Hook right arms and turn with brisk walking steps. Strike heels together on eight. Change arms and repeat. Continue through the strain of music, alternating directions, four times in all.

Measures 1–4. Step towards the centre, close with outside foot, striking heels together. Repeat, moving away from the centre. Continue through the strain of music, alternating directions, eight times in all.

Measures 5–12. Repeat second step.

Measures 1–12 and 1–4. Turning towards centre, hop and touch top of outside toe, turn away from centre, hop and touch heel. Repeat with inside foot. Continue through both strains of the music, alternating directions.

Measures 5–8. Hook right arms and turn with skipping step—hop, step, close—beginning with outside foot. Hop on inside foot, continuously.

Measures 9–12. Change arms and repeat.

REAP THE FLAX.

Formation.   Five in each line.   All face front, hands on hips.

FIGURE 1.

A.   Measure 1.   All bend forward down to left.

Measure 2.   Reap the flax by rising.

Measure 3.   Throw it to the right side.

Measure 4.   Back in starting position, hands on hips.

Measures 5–8.   Repeat.

B.   Measures 9–16.   All turn left.   The leaders' hands on hips, the others put their hands on shoulders of those standing before, and run [or use polka step] to the right in a circle back to first formation, bending deeply to the right and left.

FIGURE 2.

A.   Measure 1.   All bend forward down to right and rise.

Measure 2.   Put the flax around the hackle.

Measure 3.   Draw it from the hackle.

Measure 4.   Back in starting position.

Measures 5–8.   Repeat.

B.   Measures 9–16.   Same as Figure 1, B.

FIGURE 3.

A.   Measures 1–4.   Numbers one and four take a short step turning to numbers two and three, and taking right hands, thumb grasp, form a spinning wheel.   The leaders (numbers five) face the wheel, and with left feet tread the wheel.   The wheel with running steps moves to left.

Measures 5–8.   All take left hands, thumb grasp, and the wheel moves to right.

B.   Measures 9–16.   Same as Figure 1, B.

FIGURE 4.

A.   Measures 1–8.   Numbers one, two, three and four take right hands, thumb grasp, and the leaders run as shuttles under their arms and around each one of the four.

B.   Measures 9–16.   Same as Figure 1, B.

FIGURE 5.

A.   Measures 1–4.   The lines march up to left side of their leaders and form a large ring, dancing to left.

Measures 5–8.   Dance to right.

B.   Measures 9–16.   The leader of the first line puts hands on hips.   Others put their hands on shoulders of those standing before, forming one line.

Music is repeated while the line traverses two sides of a large square, the diagonal and the other two sides, when the line is broken again into its original fives and the first form again is resumed.

REAP THE FLAX.

D.C.

RHEINLÄNDER.

Measures 1–8. Sixteen steps walking around circle.

Measures 1–8. Sixteen steps—hop waltz—around.

Measures 9–16. Polka forward two steps—outer foot leads—lady turns under arm of man. Four times.

Measures 9–16. Start as above, but man's arms folded, lady's akimbo. After two steps she whirls away from circle two measures, while he follows with polka, stamping as he follows. Four times.

Measures 17–24. Man kneels, lady goes around him, turning around at his shoulder—four polka steps. Then both go forward four steps. Repeat

Measures 17–24. Skater's position. Both start step with right foot crossed behind, turn toward center, then two running steps and heel forward in fourth position. Step left foot behind and run outward. Repeat.

Measures 1–8. Man kneels, lady goes around him—hop waltz, then both forward four steps. Repeat.

Measures 1–8. Polka two steps forward, start on outer foot, turn with hop waltz and lady jumps up as she turns around.

RHEINLÄNDER.

LASSIES' DANCE. II.

(KULLDANSEN.)

Will you not dance?
I surely will
And we'll be dancing
With lassie.

Lassie, lassie, lassie, lassie, lassie, lass,
Lassie, lassie, lassie, lassie, lassie, lass,
Clap, we are dancing with lassie.

The women in the province Dalcarlia in Sweden are commonly called kullor (plural), kulla (singular). This dance originated in Dalcarlia, hence the name.

Formation. It is best to number the gentlemen — 1, 2, 3, 4, etc. Whatever lady the gentleman dances with during the dance will have the same number as the gentleman she happens to have as her partner.

FIGURE I.

Each gentleman invites a lady, and the couples form a ring with the ladies on the right side of the gentlemen and nearest the centre of the ring. The gentlemen face about and take one step backward, partners thus standing diagonally opposite each other. All place hands on hips, regular dancing position. Each one places right foot straight forward, turn left about face on right heel and toes of left foot and bow to the one behind, singing: "Will you not dance?" Then when the words: "I surely will" are sung, they turn about and bow to partners. At the words: "And we'll be dancing" all again face about and bow as in the beginning. When the words: "With lassie" are sung, all again turn forwards and bow to partners. Repeat. While the words: "Lassie, lassie, lassie, lassie, lassie, lass" are sung twice, all hop with springing, feet forward alternately. At the word "clap" all clap their hands once and then dance around with partners while singing: "We are dancing with lassie."

The gentlemen then take a step forward, thus changing partners.

Described by Nils Bergquist, following the original Swedish setting.

THE LASSIES' DANCE. II.

(KULLDANSEN.)

62

LASSIES' DANCE. II. (Continued.)

FIGURE 2.

Formation as before. When the song begins, gentleman and lady take right hands, left hands on hips and place left foot one step forward, heel on the floor, toes raised. Each one leans over to the left, turning slightly to the right. Next they take left hands, right foot forward, lean to the right and turn to the left. These movements alternate while the words: "Will you not dance, I surely will, And we'll be dancing, With lassie" are sung twice. The last part of the figure is the same as in figure 1.

FIGURE 3.

Formation as before. Couples one and two form a square, three and four, etc. The gentleman of each couple takes with his right hand the right hand of the lady of the other couple. The hands of the odd numbered couple is uppermost. When the first phrase is sung, all dance as in figure 2. Last part is danced as in figure 1.

FIGURE 4.

The gentleman steps behind his partner and places his hands at her waist. Ladies place hands on hips. The gentlemen place their left heels on the floor diagonally forward and lean over to the right, at the same time that the ladies place their right heels on the floor, diagonally forward, and turn backward to the right. Thus gentlemen and ladies are half turned toward each other. The position of feet and trunk are changed, as feet were changed in previous figures, while the first phrase is sung. Last part of the figure as in figure 1.

FIGURE 5.

Formation as in third figure except that couples form ring instead of crossing arms. While first phrase is sung they dance around to left, alternately placing left and right heel on the floor. Last part of the figure as before.

A RUSSIAN DANCE.

(KOMARINSKAJA.)

The Russian "Komarinskaja" is composed of an almost unlimited number of steps from which the dancer makes his own selection according to his ability or inclination. Many of these steps call for great strength and agility on the part of the dancer and are usually executed only by men.

The steps here described have been selected from a large number and simplified, so that they may be easily understood and put to practical use by men in the gymnasium.

The music, "Cerdetschni," is a Russian folk melody, having two distinct strains of eight measures each. In the description of the following steps, the count—one, and, two, and—is indicated.

FIRST STEP.

Measure 1. With the left hand on the hip, right arm extended forward, palm up and right leg extended forward, toes up, step forward with right foot, the heel touching the floor first (one), close the left foot to the right (and), step forward with right foot (two), raise the left leg forward, toes up (and).

Measure 2. Repeat same, beginning with the left foot and swinging the extended right arm across the body toward the left, palm down.

Measures 3–8. Continue alternating right and left and finish, arms folded, with three stamps in place. Left (one), right (and), left (two), pause.

In executing this step move forward and around in a circle, returning to original position where the three stamps are made. The steps should be long and skimming, the arm should be swung laterally from side to side, the head thrown back and turned toward the right, and the body turned from side to side in the direction of the swinging arm.

SECOND STEP.

Measure 9. With the arms extended step sideward with the right foot, at the same time giving a barbaric yell (one), step across behind with the left foot (and), step sideward with the right foot (two), step across behind with the left foot (and).

Measures 10–12. Continue same, moving to the right, and finish with another step sideward with the right foot (one, and), stamp the left foot across in front of the right and extend both arms diagonally downward to the left (two, and).

Described by Elizabeth Burchenal, Public Schools Athletic League, New York City.

64

Measures 13–16. Repeat beginning with the left foot and moving to the left, and finish with three stamps in place, arms folded — left (one), right (and), left (two), pause (and).

Execute this step as if running sideward, but without any up and down motion.

THIRD STEP.

Measure 1. With arms crossed diagonally downward, bend the knees, "sitting on heels" (one, and), extend the knees, at the same time springing to a stride position on heels (two, and).

Measures 2–8. Repeat, and, with arms folded, finish with three stamps in place (one), (and), (two, and).

While executing this step, progress forward.

FOURTH STEP.

Measure 9. With arms folded, head inclined to the right and right foot raised close behind the left knee put the right foot down close behind the left foot (one), raise the left boot back of the right knee, inclining the head to the left (and), put the left foot down close behind the right foot (two), raise the right foot close behind the left knee, inclining the head to the right (and).

Measures 10–16. Repeat and finish with three stamps in place (one), (and), (two, and).

Execute on the toes and as if walking backward with a springy step, and with exaggerated knee raising before each step. Take care to turn the knee out sideward in raising it.

FIFTH STEP.

Measure 1. With the arms swung sideward and up slightly above the shoulder level, and the right leg extended and raised sideward, hop on the left foot (and — last count of preceding measure), step sideward with the right foot, at the same time swinging the arms down and across each other and giving yell (one, and), step across behind with the left foot, immediately raising the right leg extended sideward and swinging the arms sideward and up (two), hop on the left foot (and).

Measures 2–4. Continue moving to the right and finish, arms folded, with three stamps in place (one), (and), (two, and).

Measures 5–8. Repeat, beginning with the left foot and moving to the left, and finish, arms folded, with three stamps in place (one), (and), (two, and).

In executing this step, move sideward even on the hop. In swinging the arms down bend the body forward, and when the arms are swung up throw back the head and look in the direction in which the step is moving. Move impatiently and cover as much distance as possible.

SIXTH STEP.

Measure 9. With the arms folded bend the right knee and sit on the right heel extending the left leg forward, the heel touching the floor and giving a yell of exultation (one, and), change weight to the left foot, sitting on the left heel, and extending the right leg forward (two, and).

Measures 10–16. Continue alternating and finish with three stamps in place (one), (and), (two, and), simultaneously with the third stamp extend the arms and throw back the head with an exultant yell.

In executing this step move forward around a circle returning to place where the three stamps are made. The yell in the step occurs only twice—at the first movement and at the final step.

CERDETSCHNI.

MONDANET MAGANAK.

First Step.

Position. Arms folded in front—held high.

Measure 1. Hop on left foot and touch right toe to side, heel up, turning body away from foot. Hop on left foot and touch right heel to side, toe up, turning body toward foot.

Measure 2. Hop on right foot and touch left toe to side. Hop on right foot and touch left heel to side.

Measures 3–8. Continue alternating sides.

Measures 1–6. Repeat.

Measures 7–8. Break. Arms folded in front. Hop right, touch left toe in front of right. Hop left, touch right toe in front of left. Hop right, touch left toe in front of right. Hold.

Second Step.

Position. Same as in First Step.

Measure 1. Right slide to right. Right cut (or kick) to right.

Measure 2. Left slide to left. Left cut to left.

Measures 3–8. Continue alternating.

Measures 1–6. Repeat.

Measures 7–8. Break as in First Step.

Third Step.

Position. Left arm in half circle above and in front.

Measure 1. Hop on left, touch right toe to right side. Hop on left, touch right heel to right side.

Measure 2. Hop on left, touch right toe in front of left. Hop on left, extend right foot obliquely forward.

Measures 3–4. Same hop right, using left foot.

Measures 5–6. Repeat alternating.

Measures 7–8. Break as in First Step.

Fourth Step.

Position. Same as in Third Step.

Measures 1–2. Mazurka right—slide right, hop left, bend right leg.

Measures 3–4. Break as in First Step.

Measures 5–6. Mazurka left.

Measures 7–8. Break as in First Step.

Measures 1–8. Repeat, start right.

Description by Bessie K. Marsh.

MONDANET MAGANAK.

MONDANET MAGANAK. (Continued.)

FIFTH STEP.

Position.   Same as in First Step.
Round Polka.   Complete turn start right.
Measure 1.   Stamp right, left, right, one-half turn.
Measure 2.   Stamp left, right, left, one-half turn.
Measures 3–4.   Break —facing forward.
Measure 5.   Stamp left, right, left, one-half turn.
Measure 6.   Stamp right, left, right, one-half turn.
Measures 7–8.   Break — facing front.

SIXTH STEP.

Position.   Same as in First Step.
Kick Step.
Measure 1.   Hop left and strike right heel to left.   Repeat.
Measure 2.   Step right to right side.   Cross step left behind.
Measures 3–4.   Repeat, continue to right.
Measure 5.   Hop left, touch right toe to right side.   Repeat.
Measure 6.   Repeat with left.
Measures 7–8.   Break.
Measures 1–8.   Repeat.

SEVENTH STEP.

Position.   Same as in First Step.
Shuffle Step.   Thirty-two counts.   Shuffle right, forward.
Measure 1.   Shuffle right and bend leg upward.   Shuffle right and extend leg
      forward.
Measures 2–3.   Break, start right, same step and shuffle left.
Measure 4.   Shuffle left, bend leg upward.   Shuffle left, extend leg forward.
Measures 5–6.   Break, same step.
Measures 7–8 and 1–4.   Repeat.
Measure 5.   Stamp right, right arm neck firm, making one-half turn right, bend
      left leg upward.   Hold last count.
Measure 6.   Same left, changing arms.
Measure 7.   Whirl right, complete turn, waving left hand.   Stamp right, stamp
      left.
Measure 8.   Repeat same direction.   Hold attitude.

THE RILL. II.

Formation.   Double circle with partners.

Measures 1–2.   Two schottishe steps beginning with outside foot.

Measures 3–4.   Dance around with four jig steps (step hop).

Measures 5–6.   Partners take right hands, free hands on hips.   Raise right arm. B turns with four jig steps under raised arm, one turn to right with four jig steps.

Measures 7–8.   Partners dance around with four jig steps.

Measures 1–8 (repeated).   B with hands on hips dances five jig steps turning one turn to right.   A follows with arms folded.   A with hands at B's waist, and B with hands on A's shoulders, dance around with four jig steps.   On last two counts, A lifts B over to their right side.

LAUDNUM BUNCHES.

Formation.   Sets of six partners facing each other.

Step One. Stamp right, left, right, hop on right and raise left knee.   Alternate feet.   With hands clinched, swing the arms vigorously down and up, starting from the upward position, on the first stamp.

Step Two. Snatch step (step hop), moving backward.   On each step the arms make a small inward circle.

1.   Corner Figure.

At the end of the introduction, numbers one and six jump in place swinging arms up to position.

Measures 1–2.   Using step one, numbers one and six change places passing on the right side.   Turn in place and advance to centre.

Measures 3–4.   Using step two twice, move backward to corner, finishing with jump.

Numbers two and five jump at same time and change places.   On finish, numbers three and four jump and change places.   On finish, all jump and take second figure.

2.   Figure 8.

Using step one, numbers two, four and six form figure 8, at the same time numbers one, three and five form figure 8.   Numbers one and two, five and six, turning outward, numbers three and four turning inward.   When 8 is half completed, all jump facing inward.   Repeat forming other half of 8, the ends starting inward, centres starting outward.   Finish as above. Using step one on measures 1 to 6, step two on measures 7 to 8.

3.   Repeat Corner Figure.

4.   Cross Over.

Using step one, opposite numbers change place.   Finish with step two in place, facing inward.   Repeat, returning to position.

5.   Repeat Corner Figure.

6.   Back to Back.

Using step one opposite numbers move half way across, pass back to back, and return to place, using step two on the return.

7.   Repeat Corner Figure.

Finish in semicircle.   Jump raise right foot and hold position, shout "hey!"

LAUDNUM BUNCHES.

RUSSIAN COSSACK DANCE.

Measures 1–4. Jump sideways with feet crossing—right, right, right and repeat.

Measures 5–8. Jump feet sideways right, double kick and three stamps, right, right, right, left.

Measures 9–12. Inching right, six counts and three stamps. Repeat left.

Measures 13–16. Toe, heel. Four times on both sides.

Measures 1–4. Move forward with feet winding movement, forward. Hands back of head.

Measures 5–8. Move backward with same movement of feet.

Measures 9–12. Toe, heel, touch front and clap foot with hand, twice on each side.

Measures 13–16. Clap hands under right leg, hopping twice on left. Same under left leg. Four times under each leg.

Measures 1–4. Move forward with arms folded in front, wiggling first right heel in front, then left heel in front, toe touching floor.

Measures 5–8. Move back with hands back of head and knee bend and kick right foot. Repeat kicking first right and then left.

Measures 9–12. Touch fingers forward to toes and jump on heels throwing arms sideways.

Measures 13–16. Move back with right hand on hip, left hand back of head and double hop on tip toes with knees high in front.

Measures 1–4. Move around in circlet to the right with inching step looking back over shoulder.

Measures 5–8. Move around in circle to left with inching step looking back over shoulder and end with a stamp forward, arms spread sideways.

RUSSIAN COSSACK DANCE.

SWEDISH POLKA.

(FJÄLLNÄSPOLSKA.)

Formation. Two lines facing each other

FIGURE 1.

Measures 1–2. Lines run forward three short steps and jump (slightly accented) on both feet.

Measures 3–4. Stamp with right foot, and swing left foot across, raise knee. Stamp with left foot, and swing right foot across, raise knee. These are called dal steps.

Measures 5–6. Run forward three more steps, and jump as before.

Measures 7–8. Repeat dal steps with right and left foot.

Measures 1–4. Couples take right hand and dance four dal steps in place, beginning with the right foot and alternating.

Measures 5–6. With a slight pull partners run past each other three short running steps, and jump to stride position with knee slightly bent, at the same time swinging both arms sideways, hands clenched.

Measures 7–8. Partners jump and face each other with same movement and repeat.

Measures 9–10. Partners again run forward three steps, passing each other and jumping to stride with bent knee.

Measures 11–12. Dance two dal steps in place, right, left,— then run forward to place and finish with two dal steps.

FIGURE 2.

Measures 13–16. Balance step, crossing right foot over left, and rising on toes. The lines move forward again. Jump and extend the right foot in point step forward, and quickly alternate left, right, left.

Measures 1–4. Repeat the balance step, beginning with left foot, then right, and alternate, point step forward as before.

Measures 5–6. Pivoting on outer heel, partners turn away from each other, at the same time touching toe in point step with other foot.

Measures 7–8. Stamp in place, backs turned toward each other, jump feet forward alternately.

Measures 1–4. Repeat balance step, right, left, and jumping feet forward.

Measures 5–8. Again repeat balance step with jumping feet forward.

SWEDISH POLKA.

(FJÄLLNÄSPOLSKA.)

Variation (of the 2d repeat).

SWEDISH POLKA. (Continued.)

(FJÄLLNÄSPOLSKA.)

INTERLUDE.

Measures 9–12.   Couples take hands, facing each other, and dance eight dal steps, right and left foot alternately.   This dal step differs from the previous, as follows : step to the right with the right foot, resting all weight on the left, swing right foot sideways.

FIGURE 3.

Measures 13–16.   Lines dance four dal steps, moving toward each other, at the same time swinging arm in a salute with every step.

Measures 1–8.   Couples meet in center, dance one turn in place, separate, and run backward three steps, and jump to stride bending knees, with arms stretching sideways.   Repeat same.

INTERLUDE.

Measures 9–14.   The gentlemen now stand behind with hands to ladies' waists, alternately bending slightly and looking over ladies' shoulder, while lady looks back.

Measures 15–16.   Gentleman dances lady around to right, one turn.

Measures 9–16.   Repeat, partners finishing back to back.

FIGURE 4.

Measures 1–6.   Lady executes a point step sideways, and beckons to gentleman opposite, who points with his right foot and declines by nodding.

Measures 7–8.   All turn once, ladies left and gentlemen right.

Measures 1–6.   The gentlemen now beckon, and the ladies decline.

Measures 7–16.   The dance finishes by the couples dancing the Hambo Polka. Right knee bent in going round, and then turn quickly on toes, left, right.

TRALLEN.

Formation. Any number of couples. Form single circle. Face center. Couples numbered from left to right in groups of fours. B on right side of A. Partners join hands, free hands on hips.

FIGURE 1.

Measures 1-8. All join hands and circle moves to left with eight three steps—ordinary short running steps, accenting first step of every three.

CHORUS.

Measures 9-16. Partners join both hands and dance around in place with four three steps to right, and with four to the left. Dancing around to right partners extend horizontally left arms, right arm bent, and dancing to left, right arms straight and left bent. Taken between each two figures.

FIGURE 2.

Measures 1-8. Starting position. Eight pas-de-basque-steps—cross balance steps—beginning left foot.

Measures 9-16. Chorus as above.

FIGURE 3.

Measures 1-8. All dance eight dal steps in place, stamping first on right foot,—stamp right foot sidewards right, swing left across right while hopping once on right, same to left.

Measures 9-16. Chorus as above.

FIGURE 4.

Measures 1-4. All face centre. "Look out position" is taken four times with A behind B.

Measures 5-8. All quickly face about and with B behind A, "Look out position" is taken four times.

Measures 9-16. Chorus as above.

FIGURE 5.

Measures 1-8. A's form inside circle facing outward, B's outside circle facing inward. Partners in front of and facing each other, take right hands and dance eight dal steps in place.

Measures 9-16. Chorus as above.

TRALLEN. (Continued.)

FIGURE 6.

Measures 1–8.   Couples place themselves behind each other forming a circle.   B on right side of A, A with right hand holding partner's left.   B outside and A inside the circle, free hands on hips.   All except couple number one bend down and clap hands in time with the music.   Couple number one raise arms forming an arch, and run around the circle, stamping on each third step.   Arch forms over the bent couples' heads, B inside, A outside.   Run to starting place where they bend forward and take same position as other couples.   As soon as couple one has passed over couple two, couple two rise and form arch and follow couple one, and all other couples do the same.   Music repeated until all have returned to places, keeping time to music by clapping.

Measures 9–16.   Chorus as above.

FIGURE 7.

Measure 1–8.   Position same as figure 6, A with right arm around partner's waist and B with hand on A's right shoulder.   Free hands on hips.   Couples dance forward in circle two dal steps, then dance around in place to left with two three steps, arms extended horizontally.   Repeat three times.

Measures 9–16.   Chorus as above.

TRALLEN.

(FJÄLLNÄSPOLSKA.)

Variation (of the 2d repeat).

THE STUYVESANT DANCE.

Sideward Leap.

Measures 1–2. Hips firm. Step left with left foot. Cross right over forward to left, face slightly to left and raise left foot behind. Hop on right in last position. Jump back to left foot, raising right.

Measures 3–4. Arm raised sideward. Step to right with right. Cross left over to right, raising right behind. Hop on left. Jump back to right foot.

Measures 5–8. Repeat.

Inching Sideways.

Measure 1. Left arm half circle over head. Inch sideways on left foot, right foot following.

Measure 2. Right arm on hip. Weight on left. Start with stamp with left on count one and bring up between counts. Look over the right shoulder.

Measures 3–4. Repeat toward right, look over left shoulder, and reverse arms.

Measures 5–8. Repeat.

Toe and Heel and Cakewalk.

Measures 9–10. Hips firm. Left foot sideward, left with heel up. Left foot sideward, left toe up. Same to right.

Measures 11–12. Repeat.

Measures 13–16. Run forward with knees high, head well back.

Measures 9–12. Repeat toe and heel.

Measures 13–16. Run back with knees high.

Knee–Twist and Side–Kick.

Measure 1. Hips firm. Knees bent, weight on left, right knee twisted in, heel turned out, instep toward floor.

Measures 2–3. Reverse position, left knee twisted. Repeat.

Measure 4. Repeat measure one.

Measures 5–8. Hop on left foot, touch right in front of left. Hop on left, kick right obliquely forward. Repeat this moving three or four inches toward left with each count.

Measures 1–4. Repeat knee-twist, beginning opposite.

Measures 5–8. Repeat side-kick, beginning opposite.

Jumping Jacks and Cobbler.

Measure 9. Jumping Jack. Right arm up. Left arm at side, right arm obliquely forward, upward on first count. Hop on bent left knee, right leg obliquely forward, heel down, toe up.

Description by Abner P. Way, M. D. The dance was developed in the Stuyvesant High School, New York City.

THE STUYVESANT DANCE.

(THE IRISH WASHERWOMAN.)

THE STUYVESANT DANCE. (Continued.)

Measure 10. Left arm up. Reverse position, left foot out.

Measure 11. Right arm up, repeat as above.

Measure 12. Left arm up, repeat as above. Right arm up, as above.

Measures 13–16. Cobbler. Jump to deep bent knees, heels together, hands straight down between knees. Jump to wide stride, heels on floor, toes up sideways, swinging arms sidewards upward to oblique. Repeat.

Measures 9–12. Repeat Jumping Jacks beginning opposite.

Measures 13–16. Repeat Cobbler beginning opposite.

SIDEWARD AND TURN.

Measure 1. Quick hop on right, raising arms and left foot sideward, leap sideward to left foot. Bring right foot across back of left and quick hop on right, arms crossed down in front.

Measure 2. Leap out to left again. Bring right across back and hop on right.

Measures 3–4. Leap to left foot, right raised backward, left arm half circle overhead, right arm down and back. Turn about left, hopping on left.

Measures 5–8. Repeat, starting toward right.

Measures 1–8. Repeat from beginning.

SINGLE KICK AND SIDE–STEP.

Measure 9. Hips firm. Hop on left, touch right across in front. Hop on left, kick right obliquely forward.

Measure 10. Quick hop on left, bring right back to left foot, weight on right. Step left a few inches to left on half-count and step right few inches to left back of left foot.

Measures 11–12. Repeat opposite.

Measures 13–16. Repeat from beginning.

DOUBLE KICK AND SIDE–STEP.

Measures 9–10. Hips firm. Hop on left foot, touch right across front. Hop on left, kick right obliquely forward. Repeat.

Measures 11–12. Quick hop on left, bring right back of left foot, weight on right, and repeat side-steps as in single kick, but twice as many steps and twice as far to right.

Measures 13–16. Repeat, starting opposite.

FINISH.

Repeat Jumping Jacks and Cobbler to the desired side until all are in column. Those already in place should do the Cobbler till all are in line.

Running Schottische = 1, 2, 3, kick.
Polka

rare
150 net
16 post.